ordered 3-17-88

THE STRENUOUS LIFE

THE STRENUOUS LIFE

The "Oyster Bay" Roosevelts
in Business and Finance

by

Wm. T. Cobb

WILLIAM E. RUDGE'S SONS

NEW YORK

I PREACH TO YOU, THEN, MY COUNTRYMEN, THAT OUR COUNTRY CALLS NOT FOR THE LIFE OF EASE BUT FOR THE LIFE OF STRENUOUS ENDEAVOR. THE TWENTIETH CENTURY LOOMS BEFORE US BIG WITH THE FATE OF MANY NATIONS. IF WE STAND IDLY BY, IF WE SEEK MERELY SWOLLEN, SLOTHFUL EASE AND IGNOBLE PEACE, IF WE SHRINK FROM THE HARD CONTESTS WHERE MEN MUST WIN AT HAZARD OF THEIR LIVES AND AT THE RISK OF ALL THEY HOLD DEAR, THEN THE BOLDER AND STRONGER PEOPLES WILL PASS US BY, AND WILL WIN FOR THEMSELVES THE DOMINATION OF THE WORLD. LET US THEREFORE BOLDLY FACE THE LIFE OF STRIFE, RESOLUTE TO DO OUR DUTY WELL AND MANFULLY; RESOLUTE TO UPHOLD RIGHTEOUSNESS BY DEED AND BY WORD; RESOLUTE TO BE BOTH HONEST AND BRAVE, TO SERVE HIGH IDEALS, YET TO USE PRACTICAL METHODS.

"THE STRENUOUS LIFE"

> —*Speech by Theodore Roosevelt before the Hamilton Club,* Chicago, April 10, 1899.

TABLE OF CONTENTS

CHAPTER I.

THE PATTERN OF A FAMILY

IN 1934 an apocryphal story began the rounds of the financial world and, embellished in the telling by one of the country's leading elder statesmen and raconteurs, finally appeared in a national publication. In its most commonly told form, it appeared that Philip J. Roosevelt, of the old New York firm of Roosevelt & Son, had addressed a letter to a descendant of "the other branch" of that name, Franklin Delano Roosevelt, President of the United States.

"In view of the Administration's attitude toward the utility industry," he was alleged to have written, "what do you suggest that we do with Mrs. Roosevelt's utility investments?" And the President was supposed to have answered, "I have nothing to suggest. Investments are your business, not mine."

Finally, the story went, another missive was sent from the somewhat austere offices of the old firm to the White House. "We have liquidated the utility investments in question," it read, "and have invested the proceeds in government bonds. Now it's your business."

However diverting this yarn may have been, even to the principals involved, its spurious nature is obvious to those who are acquainted with the stature of the firm of Roosevelt & Son. For this firm to have countenanced an important change in the investments it was handling in order to make the point of a witticism is unthinkable. Rather, the firm would go to the opposite extreme in insisting upon having

1

good, objective investment reasons for all decisions which bear on the safety and productivity of funds entrusted to its care.

Back of this rational investment policy there lies a history, a tradition and a practice, unusual even among the old conservative financial firms of New York. In the story of Roosevelt & Son and the family which has nurtured and husbanded the business for a century and a half we see symbolized to an amazing degree the pattern of America's national development.

As America changed, so did the activities of the Roosevelts. As the young country grew to maturity among the nations, first as colony, then as independent state, then as world power, so did the members of this family reflect that development. It is as logical that George Emlen Roosevelt, head of the firm today, should concentrate on the conservation and healthy growth of the property and savings that are in his care as that his Dutch ancestor, Claes Martenszen van Rosenvelt, in the 17th Century, should have farmed the land of the New World into which he had come.

Let's follow the thread of this story of ten generations of a family as it is woven into the fabric of American Life.

CHAPTER II.

Claes Martenszen van d. 1659?
Nicolaes 1658-1742

Nicolaas 1687-?   Johannes 1689-?   Jacobus 1692-1776

THE MILLER'S STORY

The Colony Finds
Its Commercial Feet

IF NICOLAES ROSEVELT, over two centuries ago, could have
looked down the vista of years to come, he would have recognized himself as one of the most distinguished of American
ancestors-to-be. But not being gifted with prescience any more
than less fortunate progenitors, he could not know that two of
the three sons who gathered about him periodically were to
become the founders of outstanding branches of an outstanding American family in commerce, statecraft and finance.

But if Nicolaes Rosevelt thought along the lines of family
at all it is more likely that his reflections drifted back to his
father, Claes Martenszen van Rosenvelt, who some eighty-five
years previously, about 1648, had come to the comparatively
hospitable shores of this country with his wife, Jannetje. Here
in the New World, Claes had established himself in the rather
wild Dutch colony of New Amsterdam, to seek the chance for
personal progress which his native land had apparently denied
him. For, in spite of the dangers of Indians, the inept governors
the Dutch sent over (except the able though choleric Peter
Stuyvesant, the incumbent when Claes arrived) and the general
uncertainties of living on the virtual border of a wilderness,
the conditions which he had left behind him in the old world
were even less happy. And he was young, not long married, and
could face a new continent with a high heart.

AN EARLY VIEW
OF NEW AMSTERDAM

PETRUS STUYVESANT
Governor of New Amsterdam when Claes Martenszen
van Rosenvelt arrived in America from Holland.

It is doubtful if even his son Nicolaes knew in detail all about his forebears in Holland, for Claes had died when Nicolaes was a baby. However, he must have known that the times had been turbulent, the Low Countries were none too peaceful, and it may well be that Claes Martenszen van Rosenvelt, as many millions did after him, left with no regrets. One ingenious genealogist, not connected with the family, has recently presented the hypothesis that a certain Marten Goldersman opt Roosevelt was the father of Claes, and that the latter's farm having been flooded by one of the inundations that afflicted the country from time to time, he became entangled financially. If this was, indeed, the circumstance, and the object of Claes' emigration was to improve his own and his children's fortunes by cutting his connections with Holland, his judgment was abundantly vindicated by three centuries.

The classic conception of the New Amsterdam in which he arrived is not in accordance with the facts. Legends, stories and plays have contrived to give 20th Century Americans a picture of a placid, even sleepy town, with a people almost exclusively Dutch, and equally exclusively devoted to long-stemmed pipe puffing, huge meal digesting, and grunting in Dutch to their equally taciturn, contented wives—the latter as industrious as they were invariably seemly in conduct.

The facts are that New York in 1648 was rather different. The Dutch were actually a minority, and English, Portuguese, Spanish, French and German expatriates strolled in the muddy lanes. Nor were the occupations of the populace always sedentary or refined; bold "privateersmen," the dividing line between whom and outright pirates was a legal nicety, openly paraded in the streets and invaded the taverns.

7

MAIDEN LANE

So named because in the early Dutch days girls did the family laundry in the stream that flowed beside it. Roosevelt & Son later had its place of business on this street.

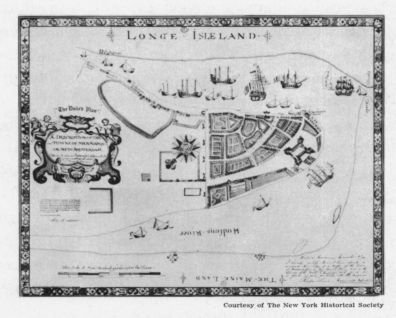

"THE DUKE'S PLAN"

Official map of New Amsterdam just before it became New York in 1664. Wall Street was so named because it ran just behind the wall which guarded the city on the north (left).

But then, as now, the spectacular phase was just the froth of New York. Solid as the bedrock on which the city stands, hardy traders with the Indians, energetic farmers and legitimate merchant sailors steadily pursued their courses. This was Claes' New Amsterdam—the New Amsterdam of which he immediately became a functioning part, as successful as many, not so sensational as some, but a vital part of the new society he helped to mold.

Claes was often known, it appears, as "Kleytjen"—literally translated as "the little one," or in the vernacular of our own day, "Shorty." Because of this fact, and certain historical references to a "Shorty" who spent many years in the New World as an adventurer, trader and trapper, it is supposed by some that this trip to the New World was not his first. However this may be, the official debut of Claes Martenszen van Rosenvelt in American records occurred on October 23, 1650, when his son Christiean, Nicolaes' elder brother who died in infancy, was baptized in the Dutch Reformed Church. In a day in which large families were not only the rule but almost required of respectable Dutch folk by public opinion, Claes and Jannetje did their duty. Five other little Rosenvelts followed their brother to baptism in the Dutch Reformed Church, but of them Nicolaes was the only other boy; consequently, the family name was carried on by him alone. This he did with a vengeance; he had ten children, of whom three were to become successful businessmen.

Now, in 1735, Nicolaes was seventy-seven years old, yet this stout, hale patriarch was to live for several years more. The America in which he lived was no longer the simple, almost entirely trading-agricultural country to which Claes had come.

Progress was in the air — particularly economic progress. Literacy was more common (New York's first newspaper had been founded ten years before) although it is worth noting that a general supreme indifference to accuracy of spelling was responsible for the variety of ways (Rosenvelt, Rosevelt and Roosevelt) in which the family name was written, then and later.

And so Nicolaes, looking around him, contemplated a town which already was pushing its way to the top of American communities, though still far from the largest of them. When Claes landed, around 1648 or '49, New Amsterdam had been but a village of 700 souls. His farm, Rose Hill — probably derived from his own name which means "Rose Field" in English — had been located about four miles from the town proper. And now New York had grown to 9,000, in those days an impressive figure for a Colonial town.

Claes, with an eye to value which most decidedly was to reappear in his descendants, had chosen about the best farming land on Manhattan Island — between the swamps to the south and the hills to the north. The children were all young when Claes died about ten years after he and his wife Jannetje arrived in this country — with Jannetje following him shortly thereafter. Part of the farm was sold by the executors to support the little orphans, and the rest of it later reverted piecemeal to the city under the financial burdens, tax and otherwise, thus placed upon it, no one in the family being old enough to work the soil.

Nicolaes must have had faith in New York, and with reason. When he had taken his canoe to seek his fortune up-river for a period of years, his journey had led him to settle at

Esopus, known to us as Kingston. He had spent his early married years in Esopus and children had been born there; he had been reasonably prosperous and so, we may conclude, his original judgment had been a sound one. But with the funds he had acquired through trading, he apparently felt that he could find greater opportunity in the expanding business of the city.

He was right again. All through the story of the Roosevelts we find that they had an almost uncanny knack of associating themselves with a major current in American economic life; and Nicolaes was no exception to the rule. Just as his father had been a farmer when farming was the real basis of American self-sufficiency, as he himself had been a trader and trapper, so now Nicolaes became a processor of commodities—a miller of the grain now being grown in increasing quantities.

The New York he came back to differed sharply from the "New Amsterdam" to which his father, Claes, had come. In 1664, when Nicolaes was six, the British had taken it in the name of the Duke of York, to whom it had been handed by that lighthearted, lightly-giving monarch of England, Charles II. The Dutch had recaptured it, with the aid of a "fifth column" in the city, in 1673; Nicolaes, then fifteen, may even have played a part in the incident. But it was just an incident; the inexorable forces of history, political as well as economic, were at work, and Dutch rule ended finally the following year.

Young Nicolaes may have been influenced to take his chances on the river by the British occupation; when he returned, it was to find an unusually sympathetic administration at work in New York. The British governors were generally no improvement on the Dutch ones, if as good; but there was little

The Dutch surrender New Amsterdam
to the British, 1664.

TRINITY CHURCH

Built in 1696, at the head of Wall Street on Broadway. This first edifice was
burned by the British in 1776, rebuilt in 1788, and torn down to make way
for the present church building in 1846.

or no discrimination against the Dutch as Dutch, and Nicolaes had thrown himself into the political as well as the industrial life of the burgeoning town.

It was he who first anglicized his name to Nicolaes from Claes, for he had been "christened in Dutch" with the form of the name that his father had borne. Perhaps even this move was designed to further his career in an English town, although in time, Dutch ancestry was to become the very badge of Knickerbocker aristocracy. He was, in fact, successful in both of the aspects of life in which his descendants were to be outstandingly, even spectacularly, accomplished — business and politics. As a businessman, he made money; in public life, he occupied the first public office of any Roosevelt in this country, that of Alderman in 1700-01.

And now, in his old age, he could look around him at his three sons, all in middle age, and all successful. Nicolaas, the eldest son, was a goldsmith and a good one. But perhaps he was more Dutch, more phlegmatic than the other two.

No doubt Nicolaes contemplated this namesake of his with satisfaction, but he could hardly have felt the paternal pride that must have been his when he considered how ably Johannes and Jacobus — often known even then by the English equivalents, John and James — were carrying on the traditions he had started.

Close associates in business and public affairs, these two, the "livelier" of the sons, as one historian has described them, were even now middle-aged and definitely "on their way." Johannes, twenty-three years before, had entered the manufacture of linseed oil, a commodity much in demand for the painting of ships and consequently profitable to one located in the boom-

13

NEW YORK'S CITY HALL

As it was in 1701. The United States Sub-treasury building stands on this site today.

SIGNATURE OF NICOLAES ROSEVELT

The first of five Roosevelts elected Aldermen of New York City
before the Revolution.

BAPTISMS IN THE DUTCH CHURCH, FROM 1697 TO 1720.		
NAME OF FATHER.	NAME OF CHILD.	DATE OF BAPTISM.
Rosevelt, Nicolaas	Isaac	June 30, 1697
Rosevelt, Nicolaas	Rachel	April 22, 1699
Rosevelt, Nicolaas	Isaac	Feb. 28, 1701
Rosevelt, Johannes	Margreta	May 8, 1709
Rosevelt, Johannes	Nicolaas	Oct. 8, 1710
Rosevelt, Johannes	Johannes	April 27, 1712
Rosevelt, Johannes	Hilletje	May 23, 1714
Rosevelt, Johannes	Olphert	Feb. 8, 1716
Rosevelt, Johannes	Jacobus	April 23, 1718
Rosevelt, Johannes	Maria	June 15, 1720
Rosevelt, Nicolaas, Jr.	Catharina	Jan. 7, 1711
Rosevelt, Nicolaas, Jr.	Hilletje	March 29, 1713
Rosevelt, Nicolaas, Jr.	Nicolaas	Feb. 6, 1715
Rosevelt, Jacobus	Johannes	August 25, 1714
Rosevelt, Jacobus	Johannes	August 21, 1715
Rosevelt, Jacobus	Nicolaas	Oct. 13, 1717
Rosevelt, Jacobus	Helena	Oct. 11, 1719
Russel, Abraham	Johannes	March 15, 1713

THE MIDDLE DUTCH CHURCH

Where the Roosevelts worshipped after it was erected in 1731. A record of the South Dutch Church (above) shows baptisms of seventeen Roosevelts in twenty-three years around the turn of the 18th Century.

ing port of New York. And five years later he had followed in his father's footsteps by becoming an assistant Alderman, and later Alderman—a post of considerable importance at the time. He had made the metal chest which was to guard the city's new charter, and if this appears a simple task today it wasn't considered so then.

Johannes was public spirited in other ways, too. Just a year before, he, with two other prominent New Yorkers of the day, had taken the Bowling Green on lease from the city for the rent of one peppercorn — a nominal rental often used in those days for a transaction in the public interest. For nine more years, he, with his associates, was to operate the Green for the benefit of the bowling set of New York—which in those days consisted of most of the local young bucks.

Jacobus, throughout his mature years, devoted time and energy to the advancement of the Dutch Reformed Church. He, with Philip Livingston, another prominent New Yorker of the time, pioneered in modernizing its practices.

There are two touchstones of permanence in any folk tradition: Church and Language. When these two are altered, a new society is born. Jacobus Roosevelt essayed to move mountains, therefore, when, fighting to stem the apparent trend of parishioners away from his place of worship toward Episcopal Trinity, he and Livingston asked for an English-speaking minister to be appointed to the new Dutch Church.

After no less than seven meetings of the ruling body of the church, the appeal was granted, the minister appointed, and the trend back to the Dutch Church began. A new era in New York was symbolized.

Achievements of Johannes included the rebuilding of part

THE CITY OF NEW YORK ABOUT 1740
Fort George in the foreground.

BOWLING GREEN
In the days of Johannes Rosevelt, leased by him and two other
gentlemen from the city for "one peppercorn."

of Fort George and serving on the Commission to strengthen the city's fortifications during the war with the French in 1744. In addition to his other business activities, Johannes branched into the manufacture of chocolate and flour, and he became prominent as a dealer in, and improver of, New York real estate—an interest which has concerned this branch of the Roosevelts to this day.

In the latter undertakings he was associated with Jacobus. Their most important joint venture, which was to have a lasting effect on the city and on their own family fortunes, was the acquisition of a large part of what was known as Beekman's Swamp.*

It was Jacobus who had pioneered in this development, and as we see them in 1735 the brothers were probably immersed in the transactions that were to result in relocating the city's tanneries and slaughterhouses—which were as unpleasant to the New York noses of the time as they were vital to the New York backs and stomachs. By moving these unsavory industries to the Swamp, the brothers made a real contribution to their city. The fact that good business and good citizenship often go hand in hand was accepted more generally then than now. This was but one of the first of a long line of such actions that were to distinguish this family for many generations.

If old Nicolaes was proud of his sons and daughters, he must also have taken plenty of satisfaction in the truly huge brood of grandchildren that surrounded him. They numbered no less than forty-five; and in spite of the many sicknesses with

* Since this book went to press, the oldest house on Manhattan, at 11 Peck Slip, near the old "Swamps," was torn down. Erected in 1725 by Jacobus Roosevelt, it had had but three owners in its 221 years of existence. When the wreckers bored into the structure of the still sturdy old place, it was discovered to be still fit for habitation, although no one had lived in it for twenty years; its old hand-hewn beams of oak were as rugged, as sound, as ever.

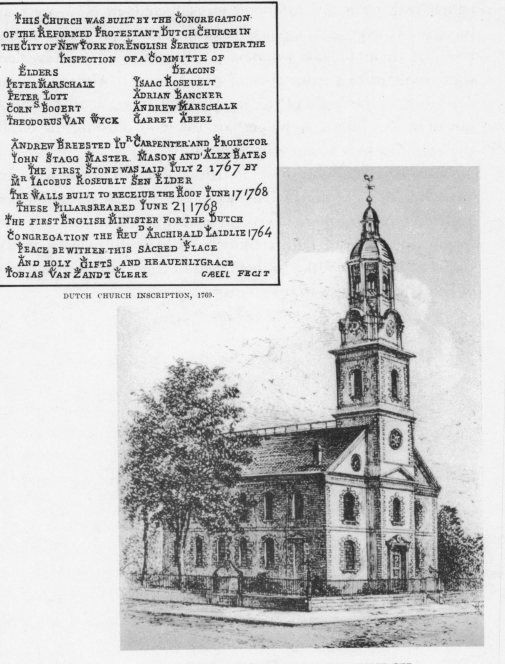

THIS CHURCH WAS BUILT BY THE CONGREGATION
OF THE REFORMED PROTESTANT DUTCH CHURCH IN
THE CITY OF NEW YORK FOR ENGLISH SERUICE UNDER THE
INSPECTION OF A COMMITTE OF

ELDERS   DEACONS
PETER MARSCHALK   ISAAC ROSEUELT
PETER LOTT   ADRIAN BANCKER
CORN.S BOGERT   ANDREW MARSCHALK
THEODORUS VAN WYCK   GARRET ABEEL

ANDREW BREESTED IUR CARPENTER AND PROIECTOR
IOHN STAGG MASTER MASON AND ALEX BATES
THE FIRST STONE WAS LAID IULY 2 1767 BY
MR IACOBUS ROSEUELT SEN ELDER
THE WALLS BUILT TO RECEIUE THE ROOF IUNE 17 1768
THESE PILLARS REARED IUNE 21 1768
THE FIRST ENGLISH MINISTER FOR THE DUTCH
CONGREGATION THE REUD ARCHIBALD LAIDLIE 1764
PEACE BE WITHIN THIS SACRED PLACE
AND HOLY GIFTS AND HEAUENLY GRACE
TOBIAS VAN ZANDT CLERK   GÆBEL FECIT

DUTCH CHURCH INSCRIPTION, 1769.

THE NORTH DUTCH CHURCH
In which Jacobus Rosevelt was Senior Elder and Isaac
Rosevelt was Deacon in 1769.

which 18th Century childhood was afflicted, in New York as in virtually every other place, most of them were alive at this time. Of them all, one wonders if two may not have revealed special qualities to the eyes of old Nicolaes: Helena, often described as the belle of the family, and Isaac, at that time a boy of nine, who was to be perhaps the most outstanding of all the 18th Century Roosevelts.

More than half of these fourth-generation Roosevelts in America, twenty-four in fact, were the sons or daughters of Johannes and Jacobus. It was these two brothers who were to be the forebears of family branches which differed in many respects, but were alike in this: each of them gave a President of the United States to his country.

CHAPTER III.

JAMES I ROOSEVELT
1759-1840

CHAPTER III.

MERCHANT OF YOUNG NEW YORK

UP, up the course of history was swinging post-Revolutionary America; every month, it seemed, brought new activity to the bustling port of New York. The city was already becoming a metropolis, as the Western World counted size; now, in 1797, upwards of 50,000 souls jammed the city. And they literally jammed it, for only seven years before the population had been less than 30,000.

Here, amid streets in which pigs, semi-official scavengers of the town, still muddied the fawn-colored trousers of the gentlemen and forced their consorts from the path; here, in a town just recovering from the first of the epidemics of "yellow jack" that were to plague it; here, just fourteen years after the end of the War of Independence, a man, a merchant and the son and grandson of merchants, had started an enterprise that was to be uninterrupted down to and including the present day.

The merchant was James I Roosevelt; the enterprise, Roosevelt & Son; its location, Maiden Lane; its first business, hardware.

James I had grown up in the period when Thomas Jefferson, Thomas Paine, Benjamin Franklin and other leaders of America's crusade for freedom were vigorously espousing a new political and economic concept for mankind. When the gathering storm clouds finally burst in 1775, the seventeen-year-old James I, along with other descendants of Johannes and Jacobus, played a part of distinction and honor.

23

James I immediately signed up in the Commissary Department of the Army, serving throughout the war without pay. His father, James, a son of Johannes, was a quiet storekeeper in a modestly successful way and no soldier by training; yet he shouldered his musket with other patriots although well into his fifties. Isaac, a son of Jacobus and a cousin of James I, became a national figure.

Many men of property and position hesitated to risk everything for a cause, and some became the outstanding Tories of New York, but Isaac Roosevelt never wavered, giving his property, his money and his services without stint to the struggle for Independence.

A State Senator during the war and serving, though over fifty years of age, in the County Militia during the actual fighting, he was among those who later campaigned for adoption of the State Constitution. As a lieutenant of Alexander Hamilton and consequently an outstanding Federalist, he helped fight and win for the cause of his leader and his party at the epochal State Convention that ratified the Constitution of the United States.

His career as a businessman was no less enterprising and significant. His had been the first sugar mill in New York; his name was among the founders of the Chamber of Commerce; and, perhaps most important, he served on the first Board of Directors of the Bank of New York and was that institution's second President, two years after it was founded in 1784.

The importance of this bank to a country that was bursting from the chrysalis of colonialism was, of course, enormous. It was not only the first bank to be organized in New York, but the second in this country; its existence opened greater horizons to businessmen who were, like James I Roosevelt in 1797, implanting themselves firmly in the nation's growing economy.

Three years before, Isaac had died, full of honors bestowed by his fellow citizens from Washington down. A new generation was trying its wings in a favorable atmosphere of peace and unfettered private enterprise. James I had gained a knowledge of the hardware business and had established substantial trade contacts by working with his father in the years immediately following the war. Also he had saved money. Thus he was well prepared, at the very beginning of the Mercantile Age in America, to strike out in a larger sphere than his father had ever encompassed.

His new hardware establishment on Maiden Lane was to become increasingly a large-scale enterprise; later, importation of European, particularly Dutch, materials was embarked on, and this in turn was to lead the firm into the building supply field in booming, expanding America—an expansion that, as far as New York City in particular was concerned, was to continue with but brief interruptions through the whole century to come.

A younger brother of James I, Nicholas, likewise sought to create a fortune out of the opportunities offered by the times. Nicholas was engaged in running a foundry shop over in New Jersey, across the river, a venture in which he had established himself as one of the foremost engineers of a day long in advance of the technical era. Having worked on the idea of a steamboat ever since he had been just a boy "refugee" from the British in a place of safety "up-river," he was able to offer an essential improvement to Robert Fulton, then in the midst of

The Continental Army enters
New York after the Revolution.

THE WALTON MANSION
Where the Bank of New York, first bank in the city and second in
the United States, was founded in 1784. Isaac Rosevelt was a
founder and the second President.

Steamboat "New Orleans"

Designed, built and sailed down the Mississippi by Nicholas Roosevelt, the brother of James I.

The first BANK OF NEW YORK building on present location. Corner of WILL & WILLIAM STS. Corner stone laid June 22, 1797

Two typical views of old New York when James I Roosevelt,
founder of the firm of Roosevelt & Son, started the business in
1797. The print at the top shows Federal Hall on Wall Street
at the head of Broad Street.

his experimentations. But Fulton, who later came to recognize this idea as correct, rejected it at the time.

Ultimately, Nicholas' great technical abilities and knowledge were to get some recognition when he made the first voyage down the Mississippi by steam in a vessel of his own design — terrorizing the Indians, scraping bottom on occasion, and astounding the riverfolk by proving that a steamship could go upstream as well as down — eventually arriving safely in New Orleans with his ship, his wife Lydia, and a son born during the fourteen days of this perilous pioneer voyage.

Neither Nicholas nor his careful, far-sighted brother could have known in 1797 that the inventive genius was never to make any money from his discoveries and development work on the steamboat, nor even to receive public credit for it until many years later. Indeed, if James I and Nicholas talked things over when the younger brother came to visit the newly established place of business, it may have seemed to the merchant that this was indeed a tortoise-hare relationship. But Nicholas was later to pass from the pages of history, like many other inventors and pioneers, without the reward that was so rightfully his. And it was James I Roosevelt who was to achieve the more lasting results.

The practices which were ever after to guide this branch of the family were even then cast in the mold. In successive generations, one son was always to head the financial and commercial interests of this branch of the family through the firm; and it is probable that James I even then was helping to care for the real estate interests of his father, James, then seventy-three years old, who had inherited them in turn from Johannes of the "Beekman Swamp."

The building on Maiden Lane in which Roosevelt & Son was
founded — taken many years later, probably during the time of
C. V. S. Roosevelt.

James I had married at thirty-five, late in life for those days, Maria Van Schaack, of an ancestry as Dutch as his own — a daughter of a prominent "up-river" family. And even now, in 1797, toddling about the house on Maiden Lane, was a boy of three — Cornelius Van Schaack Roosevelt. This youngster was destined to take the firm out of its swaddling clothes during the first half of the 19th Century in which the young Republic was to burgeon commercially, industrially, and financially.

CHAPTER IV.

CORNELIUS VAN SCHAACK ROOSEVELT
1794-1871 — as a young man.

OLD SUGAR HOUSE & MIDDLE DUTCH CHURCH
Liberty St. N.Y. 1830

Valentine's Manual

CHERRY ST
From the Corner of Rose

THE FLY MARKET, ON MAIDEN LANE AT PEARL STREET, AS IT WAS IN 1816.
From a lithograph by George Hayward after a drawing by J. Evers, published in *Valentine's Manual* for 1857.

SCENES IN OLD NEW YORK AROUND 1830

Rosevelt Street, mentioned in the lithograph to the left, was named after Johannes and Jacobus
a century before. It ran from the "Beekman Swamp" district toward the East River.

AN OUTSTANDING VIEW OF NEW YORK
about 1830

BROADWAY
Looking northward toward City Hall, about 1825.

CHAPTER IV.

"C.V.S."
AND THE ROARING FORTIES

"THE noises of history," said Victor Hugo, "are the sound of wooden sabots going up, and silken slippers coming down, the stairway of time."

By 1844 the wooden sabots that Claes Martenszen van Rosenvelt must have worn in his youth had indeed mounted the stairs. Cornelius Van Schaack Roosevelt, his great-great-great-grandson, sixth of his line in America, continued the steady climb. Later Roosevelts were to prove that in this case, as in those of a few other families of inherent conservatism fortified by traditional sound business practice, the latter part of Hugo's aphorism need not be valid.

The New York of the eighteen-forties had entered on a period of expansion in population, wealth and commerce that, to quote one authority, "has scarcely been equalled before or since." The average increase in population in each of the first four decades since 1800 had equalled the entire number of inhabitants of the city in that year; the ideal harbor and the great inland waterways combined to draw trade and commerce from the lusty West and agricultural South on one hand and Europe on the other. Already New York's financial facilities had been developed to such a high point that, even after the domestic waterways lost their primary function to the railroads, the city continued its financial and commercial leadership of the nation.

35

For this was the era in which the West was opening up in earnest; all through the great Central States the cities that had sprung into being during the first four decades were growing toward the greatness they have since attained: yet rich as the country was, it lacked many things that were luxuries but becoming, ever-increasingly, necessities. Among them was plate-glass.

This was the product in which the firm of Roosevelt & Son was to do most of its early business. Four years before, old James I Roosevelt had died, but even before then, C.V.S., as Cornelius was known, had helped to mold the policies of the firm. Again we see the family acumen manifesting itself; the trend of the times, plus the firm's ability to take advantage of it, had helped make James I a rich man, as is indicated by the fact that a few years later C.V.S. was estimated to be worth $250,000 and James I the younger, his brother, $150,000, much of it inherited. As a standard of comparison with present-day values, a man's daily wage in 1842 averaged from fifty to seventy-five cents.

The source of this wealth had been profits from the business, added, of course, to the increased value of the family's real estate interests. But there had been no question of sitting still and letting the growth of nation and city build their fortunes for them. All had not been "beer and skittles," even in that boom time.

The "Great Fire" of the mid-thirties had devastated downtown New York—right where many of the Roosevelt family properties were still located. Seven hundred buildings had been burned; loss was catastrophic. And two years after that, the great Panic of '37 had swept the country, and its impact was nowhere greater than in New York. Other financial crises there had been and would be, but, relatively at least, none was more drastic in its effect than this. Yet the firm had weathered the storms easily. One reason may have been that C.V.S., according to a contemporary historian, "introduced in business the principle of giving out no notes."

Now in middle life, eminently successful, C.V.S. may well have sat down to "Sunday lunch" with equanimity. The "rule" of this meal was that Dutch be spoken throughout. It was perhaps the only occasion during the week on which the ancestral language was commonly used; but now the rule was inflexibly enforced. For this had been the practice in his own youth, and his father had doubtless acquired the custom from *his* father; and back in the days of Nicolaes and even Johannes, it was probably the more comfortable language to speak, very fitting to the solid comforts of the table.

Perhaps James I Roosevelt, the clever lawyer brother of C.V.S., and his beautiful wife may have taken this occasion to "visit." James I was just about to go abroad again, this time to investigate the practice of courts of law in England, France and Holland. In the career of this Roosevelt another of the family's hereditary talents—that for public life—came to the fore. A Congressman for the two preceding years, he had declined renomination and a virtual certainty of re-election. Previously, as a member of the New York Board of Aldermen in his youth, he had taken a recess from city politics in 1830 to go abroad, where he had found and won his bride. At one time he had been leader of the New York City faction in the State Legislature; later he was to be Justice of the State Supreme Court, Judge of the State Court of Appeals and to

In 1829, looking toward Trinity Church. The New York Stock Exchange today is located on the site of the building occupied by "C. Pool, Law Books," when this drawing was made.

A view from Trinity Church, five years later.

In 1850. Note the growth of the banks and mercantile establishments, which were already giving the street its character, as contrasted with the same scene two decades earlier.

WALL STREET

hold other important posts in public life.

The "I" in his name was merely an identifying symbol, which his father had been the first to utilize as a distinguishing mark while *his* father, James, was alive. When asked by a contemporary if it stood for Isaac, James I replied: "No, it stands for I—me!"

No less a person than the aged General Lafayette gave away the bride, Cornelia Van Ness, when she was married in Paris to this distinguished American. This typifies the circles in which James I Roosevelt moved; he was a cosmopolitan gentleman of two continents, who when not engaged in public affairs at home had *entrée* abroad. At the more conservative and sedate table of C.V.S. he doubtless appeared a glamorous figure to the merchant's five sons.

These sons at this time, 1844, ranged in age from twenty-one to thirteen. C.V.S. had ample assurance that the traditions and growing worth of Roosevelt & Son would be carried on after him.

This was doubly important because the firm's business was expanding. Now Roosevelt & Son had connections with companies and banks abroad, in Holland and Switzerland notably. It is possible that James I may have had a hand in this but it was essentially the work of C.V.S.

One other James, of a very different type, may have called on this Sunday. This was James Henry, a first cousin of C.V.S. and James I. Early in life he had planned a legal career, but infantile paralysis struck him down. A double tragedy was involved, for the dread disease blighted not only his career but a romance with the lovely girl to whom he was engaged. Neither ever married.

41

New York, looking south from Union Square

The home of C.V.S. Roosevelt was on the South side of the Square on the corner of Broadway—
directly behind the large tree at the apex of the park oval.

The old Merchant's Exchange in mid-century

Where many of the leading figures of the day met to transact
important business. The Merchant's Exchange was on
Wall Street.

The North Dutch Church in 1859 — by this time
surrounded by the growing, sprawling city.

ARRIVAL OF THE MONSTER STEAMER "GREAT BRITAIN"

Thousands rushed to the Battery, at the foot of Manhattan, to observe the answer to a great problem of the time: Whether a steamer of the magnitude and construction of the "Great Britain" could make a successful trip across the ocean.

DESTRUCTION OF THE "TRIBUNE" OFFICE

A blizzard on February 4th and 5th defied all efforts to drag New York's fire-fighting equipment through the streets.

SLEIGHRIDING IN NEW YORK

After the blizzard, which drifted six feet of snow in the streets and partly demolished twenty brick houses on 26th Street.

THREE NEWSWORTHY EVENTS IN NEW YORK IN 1845

Courtesy of the New York Life Insurance Company

But thousands of others were to benefit from the results of James' affliction. He had been left a modest fortune by his father, and this he resolved to build into a fund for the sick poor of New York, who lacked the medical aid of which he had been so conscious a beneficiary. He husbanded his capital, and denied himself not only luxuries but everything above the bare necessities, and invested shrewdly in more New York real estate. When he died in 1863 he left over a million dollars to found the great Roosevelt Hospital in New York; and by the time the hospital was actually opened in 1871 this fund had grown to two millions.

James Henry's austere, idealistic way of life must have earned him the respect of C.V.S. and his sons. If so, the good opinion must have been mutual, for later events showed that the far-seeing James had, in death, turned to this cousin to be Trustee of the institution. Actually, C.V.S. himself died in 1871 — with the result that one of his sons, James Alfred, was the hospital's first President. The interest of the successive heads of Roosevelt & Son in the institution, as officers and trustees, has continued down to this very day.

In 1844, however, C.V.S. Roosevelt was thinking of other things; of the Chemical Bank, for instance, of which he was a founder and one of the five original Directors.

This institution was an off-shoot of a mercantile firm, with which C.V.S. had had business dealings for twenty years. Its development into a bank was indicative of the far greater need for finance as a handmaiden of commerce than it was in the days when Isaac helped found the Bank of New York; it was only natural that C.V.S. should have thought of the expanding needs of Roosevelt & Son in connection with the new bank.

ROOSEVELT HOSPITAL

As it looked a few years after it opened its doors in 1871 as a consequence of the bequest of James Henry Roosevelt (above). The private pavillion and ward building (below) were added many years later. A member of the firm of Roosevelt & Son has been an officer and trustee of the hospital since its founding.

And the family instinct for the sound choice, the sound action, was again demonstrated in the event; the Chemical never failed to pay its obligations in gold, even during the War Between the States, and it was the only bank in New York to make this record. Since C.V.S. was a Director during this period, we must credit the determining decisions made in the Directors' meetings in part, at least, to this sturdy, conservative old Dutchman.

It is among the ironies of history that posterity often remembers less of a man's accomplishments than of his relationship to a more illustrious individual. We may doubt that C.V.S., back there in 1844, thought much about the opinion of posterity; but if he could have envisioned the future, he probably would have been surprised to learn that he would be remembered primarily not for his accomplishments, which were real and substantial if unspectacular, but because he was the founder of what we know today as "the Oyster Bay Roosevelts" and the first Presidential grandfather in the Roosevelt family: for the immortal "Teddy" was his grandson.

CHAPTER V.

JAMES ALFRED ROOSEVELT

ROOSEVELT & SON, BANKING AND REAL ESTATE

ROOSEVELT HOSPITAL.   V.-PRES. CHEM. NAT. BK.

The third head of Roosevelt & Son.

Cornelius Van Schaack 1794-1871

| Silas Weir | James Alfred | Cornelius Van Schaack, Jr. | Robert Barnwell | Theodore |
| 1823-1870 | 1825-1898 | 1827-1887 | 1829-1906 | 1831-1878 |

CHAPTER V.

SONS

American Finance Comes of Age

NEW YORK toward the close of the seventies — just before the dawn of the Mauve Decade — was alive with the energy which it in part derived from, in part contributed to, the expanding continent that lay behind it.

Today we think of the eighties as a settled time, covering it with the patina of our nostalgia for things secure, things established and fixed. Yet it was, in fact, a time of building, a time of opportunity unparalleled in its scope. In this national industrial expansion, finance played a greater part than ever before, and there was a reason.

As an aftermath of the War Between the States, industry and agriculture had boomed enormously; in spite of setbacks, the basic urge toward expansion was still felt in the land. The corporation, as a form of enterprise, was increasingly important, and with the rise in corporate activity there came a proportionately greater need and opportunity for public financing.

Now, in 1879, the firm of Roosevelt & Son took a new course, in which James Alfred Roosevelt, the second son of C.V.S., was the guiding genius. For some time the financing of business had played an increasing part in the affairs of Roosevelt & Son. The banking, transportation and insurance responsibilities of the family were taking an increasingly large share of its attention. And, as finance at last began to come into its own in America, the importation and distribution of plate glass, the

49

STOCK EXCHANGE	PARK STREET
BRIDGE OVER BROADWAY AT FULTON	BROADWAY FROM METROPOLITAN HOTEL
FIVE POINTS	FIFTH AVENUE FROM MADISON SQUARE

"Iconography of Old New York"— Stokes

SIX NEW YORK SCENES

Shortly before Roosevelt & Son abandoned the plate-glass business to devote its entire time to the investment banking business in 1878.

firm's basic business for the three preceding decades, was becoming less and less important. The last big deal in plate glass in which the firm took part was a consequence of the Chicago fire; for the indiscretion of Mrs. O'Leary or her cow caused a tremendous demand for all construction materials. Subsequently, the very process which was causing an increase in the need for public financing—the surge toward world leadership of American industry, with expansion in fields previously dominated by European manufacture—spelled final decline of foreign plate-glass sale in America. At last Roosevelt & Son abandoned the plate-glass business altogether, and concentrated its activities in the field of banking and investment.

America had settled on a monetary course from which it was not to turn for many decades. Last of the major nations of the Occident to abandon bimetalism, the country had finally established gold as its standard, a prerequisite to full international economic development.

For some decades past, foreign investors had taken a small but increasing interest in American enterprise; and during this same period, the Roosevelt firm built important connections abroad, and these frequently involved substantial credit. Now these European contacts were to stand the firm in good stead. For in years to come, foreign — notably Dutch and Swiss — investors were to be active purchasers of senior securities sponsored by Roosevelt & Son. As time passed, the confidence of these investors in the judgment of the firm grew, and the firm of Roosevelt & Son was to be long prominently identified with the sale abroad of bonds of important American enterprises.

Again we see the family pattern interestingly repeating itself: James Alfred had entered the firm, as had brother Theodore, before the age of twenty-one. As partners, these young men had assumed responsibilities not usually held by business-men until much later in life; in consequence, their whole background was in the direction of conservatism. Likewise, in 1879, James Alfred's two sons, Alfred and William Emlen, became fully responsible, active partners of the firm, when but twenty-three and twenty-two years of age. The background of the latter, who was to head Roosevelt & Son during many of its more important years, was thus steeped in finance alone, with-out regard to the mercantile activities which had been the partial preoccupation of earlier Roosevelts.

Because of their inherently conservative attitude, neither the firm nor its principals had been crippled by the ill-fated attempt of Jim Fiske to corner gold, culminating in "Black Friday" of 1869, nor by the more serious Panic of '73, which brought low so many old houses.

James Alfred Roosevelt not only was head of the firm; in addition, he had succeeded his father on the Chemical Bank's Board of Directors and as President of the Broadway Improve-ment Association, a family real estate holding company. His directorships included the Delaware & Hudson Canal Co. and many insurance companies, including the New York Life.

Yet this quiet man, less known to posterity than either of two of his brothers, did not confine his activities to business and finance. He knew and accepted his civic responsibilities. At this time he was a Trustee of the S.P.C.C. and of the Bank for Savings; and, of course, he continued as President and financial counsellor of Roosevelt Hospital. Later he was to serve as Park Commissioner, but this comparatively minor if useful post was the only time he yielded to requests to undertake public office. For he was, first and last, at this time and throughout his long and constructive life, primarily the businessman, the financier, the careful, able guardian of the family's material interests.

And in this field he made his mark. He was an extremely close friend of James J. Hill, the great railroad builder. As a consequence of this intimate association, it was Roosevelt & Son which marketed the first issue of railroad bonds ever sold by Hill. And this was but one, if the best known, of many such undertakings by the firm under James Alfred's leadership in which the motive frankly was private profit; the result, public good.

These transactions were consummated in the firm's offices at what is now 30 Pine Street (where Roosevelt & Son is located today) but they were largely planned in the Opera Club. The opera was new to New York; however, then as now, families of position supported it, but the male members of the family didn't necessarily listen to it. This was the case with Messrs. Roosevelt and Hill who, with another crony, the financier John S. Kennedy, would foregather at the Club to indulge their real interest, the great dreams of creative enterprise, while their spouses in the boxes upheld their families' reputation for appreciation of classical music.

Hill, Kennedy and many other illustrious figures of the period moved in and out of the house at 4 West 57th Street which this Roosevelt, with that eye to New York real estate characteristic of the family, had built when the address was far north of the center of Gotham fashion. Shortly after this time, James Alfred was to build, at 804 Fifth Avenue, the first private house built on "The Avenue" above 59th Street.

New York in the eighties.

"UNCLE THEE"
At the prime of his career.

But if "Jim" Hill liked and was liked by James Roosevelt, Jay Gould did not and was not. It was Gould who made the Erie Railroad known as "The Scarlet Woman of Wall Street." There are many instances of carriers feeling the effects of his hand until this day. What we know of the characters of the two men lends credibility to the legend that James Alfred Roosevelt once had Gould thrown out of his office bodily.

Later, James Alfred was to pioneer in the financing of cable communication in the Western World; although he was too young to have participated businesswise when the first transatlantic cable was laid, the impression this enormous advance in communication made upon him must have been deep. For, as a Director and "financial man" of Central and South American Cables he was to be a key figure in extending this vital service in our hemisphere, in association with James A. Scrymser.

Two of his four brothers, Silas Weir and C.V.S., Jr., were basically like himself—interested primarily in business and only incidentally in public life. The other two, however, followed the established Roosevelt tradition of participating in public affairs. During the preceding year, 1878, Theodore had died while in the very middle of a fight against one of the corrupt political machines that influenced the times. He was in every sense appropriately the father of that famous son who was to coin the phrase, "The Strenuous Life," and so well exemplify it in his own strenuous career. For Theodore had been a hard and successful worker in the firm, and equally tireless in the pursuit of his responsibilities to his city and his nation.

During the War Between the States, he had joined in

In this late 19th Century picture of New York, the shape and general contours of the Financial District as we know it are clearly foreshadowed.

"Uncle Bob"

The distinguished Robert Barnwell Roosevelt, sportsman, lawyer, pioneer in conservation and life-long advocate of clean government.

organizing the Union League Club; had served on the Allotment Commission and undertaken numerous other patriotic activities, some at the request of President Lincoln; and was instrumental in raising regiments of New York troops. Nor when, after the war, all too many forgot, was he forgetful. At "Uncle Thee's" house the Soldiers' Employment Bureau was organized, and he was a leader of those who established the Protective War Claims Association which helped collect veterans' pay without compensation.

As a philanthropist he was unceasing in his efforts. While James Alfred was President of the Roosevelt Hospital, Theodore was a founder of the Orthopaedic. He was President of the State Board of Charities, and headed other similar enterprises. His own sons were devoted to him, as he to them. His fondness for youth went beyond the confines of his own family and he gave heavily and often of his money and time to the Newsboys' lodging houses and the Y.M.C.A. Theodore's interest in culture is typified by his directorship of the Metropolitan Museum of Art; and his versatility by the fact that he was not merely concerned with things of the city, but of nature as well, as indicated by the support he gave to the Museum of Natural History, and by his own sustained interest in outdoor life.

In this latter respect, as in his zeal for clean government, he was largely responsible for the character of his son and namesake, the President-to-be—Theodore Roosevelt.

It was said of the senior Theodore after his death: "A man of prodigious industry, the most valiant fighter of his day for the right, and the winner of his fights."

The remaining brother, Robert Barnwell Roosevelt, was similar in character and was perhaps even more outstanding in public affairs. This lawyer of the family had a love of wild life and was an authority on the subject. The author of several books, his knowledge of the outdoors was matched by his devotion to it, for he founded the New York State Fishery Commission, which has served as the model for other states, and served on it for twenty years. Many an Izaak Walton of today owes his day's sport in large part to "Bob" Roosevelt, of whom he may never have heard.

A fiery crusader, he had been one of those principally responsible for finally smashing the Tweed Ring a few years before, and in this cause edited "The Citizen" for years. He had served in Congress as an anti-Tammany Democrat, and was at this time a Commissioner of the Brooklyn Bridge, an enterprise close to the hearts of all New Yorkers. The real highlight of his career came the following year, 1880, when he was appointed Minister to the Netherlands by Grover Cleveland. It may be supposed that his boyhood attendance at "Sunday lunch" at the table of C.V.S. had so familiarized him with the language, which he spoke fluently, that his work at the Hague was at least facilitated.

There are two keys to the character of this man, of a type too rarely found in public life: the first is that, conscious of his ancestry, he founded and was first President of the Holland Society and served in a similar capacity in the Sons of the American Revolution; the second is that he was not above serving as a New York Alderman, even after being Minister and holding other posts, for precisely the same reason: in Europe this reason would have been called *noblesse oblige;* in America it was simply honor and civic duty.

It is a quality which sometimes endures in families. . . .

58

CHAPTER VI.

WILLIAM EMLEN ROOSEVELT
Fourth head of Roosevelt & Son, at the height of his career.

Silas Weir		James Alfred		Theodore	
1823-1870		1825-1898		1831-1878	
James West	Hilborne Lewis	Alfred	William Emlen	Theodore 1858-1919	
1858-1896	1849-1886	1856-1891	1857-1930	(26th President of the U. S.)	

CHAPTER VI.

OYSTER BAY

LONG ISLAND has changed vastly in the years since the Roosevelts first built summer residences there. But the part of Oyster Bay in which the Roosevelt houses still cluster is not so different, even now, from the time in which "Uncle Thee," driving his four-in-hand at a furious pace, woke up the town when his forward pair jumped a "No Passing!" sign before it was seen and the equipage brought to a halt with a crash. Wooded hills tumble in uneven cascades to the blue Sound; only a few narrow roads wind among them. Occasional driveways reveal vistas of the principal houses of the district — so often with the surname "Roosevelt" on the wooden marker near the entrance to the estate. From the windows of many of these houses you can see the whitecaps tossing on a windy day, just as "C.V.S.," first of his line to build and die in Oyster Bay, saw and fell in love with them.

Even the names are evocative: famed "Sagamore," the home of President Theodore Roosevelt, near which he lies buried; "Yellowbanks," where James Alfred lived, and the summer place, in turn, of his son, William Emlen, and today, of the latter's son, John Kean Roosevelt; "Waldeck," the home of Silas Weir Roosevelt's son, James West Roosevelt; "Old Orchard," the stately, beautiful Georgian home of Mrs. Theodore Roosevelt, Jr., widow of the famed general who died on the beaches of France during World War II; "Dolonor," the coun-

61

SAGAMORE
Home of President Theodore Roosevelt. His grave is on the top of a hill overlooking Oyster Bay and Long Island Sound.

OLD ORCHARD
The stately Georgian home in Oyster Bay of Mrs. Theodore Roosevelt, Jr., widow of the famed general who died on the beaches of France during World War II.

GRACEWOOD
The home in Oyster Bay of the present head of Roosevelt & Son, George Emlen Roosevelt.

DOLONOR
The Oyster Bay residence of Mrs. Philip James Roosevelt, the
widow of William Emlen's youngest son.

try house of Mrs. Philip James Roosevelt, the wife of another of William Emlen's sons: "Tranquility" and "Mohannas," the homes of still other Roosevelts; and, with its charming view of the little harbor and beyond it, the Connecticut shore looming on the horizon on clear days, "Gracewood"—the place of the present head of Roosevelt & Son, George Emlen Roosevelt.

Thus it was, too, when, just after the turn of the century, Theodore Roosevelt, "Cousin Thee" to the family, occupied the White House.

William Emlen Roosevelt, the then Vice-President's first cousin, had been at Buffalo with his family at his cousin's express invitation to see the opening of the Buffalo Exposition. He and his young son, George Emlen, were, therefore, present when Theodore Roosevelt was sworn in as President a few days later in that city, following the tragic assassination of President McKinley.

Theodore and William Emlen were closer than most first cousins, even though their walks of life diverged. William Emlen's only activity or interest in politics was to support Theodore's candidacies in that great American's successive campaigns for public office. Theodore, whose big-game hunting, and activities as a biographer, naturalist, and advocate of national conservation left him little time for concentration on his own material problems, in his turn respected the financial sagacity of "Cousin Emlen" who was his financial adviser before, during, and after his two terms as President.

This reliance was the more natural in that William Emlen Roosevelt had become head of the firm of Roosevelt & Son on the death of his father. It was in the very month and year that Colonel Teddy, at the head of his Rough Riders, led the famous charge up San Juan Hill. William Emlen was himself an officer of the New York National Guard, as he had been for many years, and only the precipitate end of the five-month war prevented him from joining his more famous cousin in the fight against "the Dons."

William Emlen not only discharged capably the enlarged responsibilities of the family and of the firm which devolved upon him alone, since his brother, Alfred, had preceded James Alfred in death; but he was also active in his own right in many respects.

He sat on the Boards of the Chemical Bank, the old Astor National and Gallatin National Banks, and later the Central Hanover and the Bank of New York. He actively directed several institutions and corporations.

The railroad reorganizations that had made his father one of the best known figures in Wall Street were no longer a dominant feature of finance after William Emlen became head of the firm. Just as *transportation* had been the key to America's growing economy in the 19th Century, so *communication* was vital to the country in the early part of the 20th Century. Again we see the curious Roosevelt knack of getting into a main economic current, for it was with communications that this Roosevelt was prominently identified in the latter part of his career.

Picking up the threads of his father's leadership in the field, he directed the Central and South American Cables Company prior to its acquisition by All-America Cable Company; then took the leadership of the latter as Board Chairman. When this company, in turn, was purchased by International Telephone and Telegraph Company, he became a Director of it.

The first known realization of New York's famed "Skyline" — about 1896.

WILLIAM EMLEN ROOSEVELT
ROOSEVELT & SON, BANKING AND REAL ESTATE
DIRECTOR IN MANY CORPORATIONS

Courtesy of Mr. George Emlen Roosevelt

Father of the present head of the firm, as a young man.

Another cousin of William Emlen, who died twelve years before James Alfred, was Hilborne Lewis Roosevelt—a man whose talents and inclinations were as unlike those of most of the Roosevelts as was his given name. He was a technician, the first of prominence in this branch of the Roosevelts since Nicholas the Inventor, the brother of James I the first, back in the days of the firm's infancy.

Hilborne Lewis Roosevelt was originally attracted to music; he later became interested in organs and especially in electrical possibilities as applied to that instrument. This led him, after becoming a successful manufacturer of organs, to further investigations in the electrical field, where he attained a certain celebrity. He met Alexander Graham Bell, and was associated with the launching of the telephone as a practical instrument in New York. Not only as pioneer *entrepreneur,* but as technician as well, his services were of the first importance in this connection, for he was the inventor of the automatic switch hook—perhaps the most important single improvement, from the standpoint of practical use of the instrument itself, in the long history of telephony. His premature death at thirty-seven cut short a most promising career.

Hilborne's uncle, James Alfred, and later William Emlen, his cousin, closely followed these developments in telephony and their own interest in communications was stimulated by the activities of this talented relation.

William Emlen emulated his father and grandfather in the matter of charities. He was President of the Roosevelt Hospital and a director or an officer of many other charities. Yachtsman, horseman, and devoted enthusiast of Oyster Bay and all that it offered, his interest in New York was not the less,

67

and the Roosevelt instinct for sound real estate values in the city came out in the important Park Avenue development.

New York still was largely undeveloped above 59th Street, even in the days just before the passing of James Alfred. When his son, William Emlen, visited the parental house at 804 Fifth Avenue with his three boys for the still traditional "Sunday lunch," goats grazed just a block or two away; indeed, this home of one of the civic and financial leaders of New York was on the edge of the "shanty-town" that always clusters on the outskirts of America's cities.

In those days, nearby Park Avenue real estate had little value, since the railroad ran down a cut in the center of the street. When, a few years later, electrification made covering the tracks possible, a different situation resulted. Foreseeing this development, William Emlen acquired property in the very area that was to be among the most high priced of all New York residential realty.

Steeped in the family tradition, this New York financier, who might have stepped out of a novel by William Dean Howells, was diligent in maintaining the contacts abroad that his predecessors had built up. And he well justified the confidence that these investors showed in him.

William Emlen was to live many long and useful years after the days when this branch of the Roosevelt family became forever identified with the town of Oyster Bay, and Oyster Bay itself became nationally known. He did not die until 1930, when the New York and the nation he had known in his youth had changed so dramatically that he could scarcely have recognized his surroundings had he not spent his life amid those changes and been instrumental in making many of them.

When William Emlen was a boy, the firm's offices had been at 30 Pine Street. Before he attained middle age, they were moved to the Mechanics and Metals National Bank Building at what was then 33 Wall Street; and long before his death, when the Mechanics and Metals building was torn down to make way for the J. P. Morgan & Company building, they moved back to 30 Pine.

It is typical of the Roosevelt sense of continuity and tradition that when the offices were moved back to 30 Pine, after a hiatus of decades, care was taken to see that the very desks were located on the approximate spot where they had been in *another building* when Roosevelt & Son last occupied the premises!

It was the last move of the firm — completing a total of but three locations in 150 years! Very unlike the popular conception of New York change and bustle — but, in fact, true to the actual customs of the old families and firms of the city which, like the Roosevelts, have pursued the serious, conscientious way that has helped make New York the metropolis of the world and, today, its financial center.

CHAPTER VII.

From the chief
to his lieutenant.
Theodore Roosevelt
Thanksgiving day, 1912

An early portrait of President Theodore Roosevelt with his young cousin,
George Emlen Roosevelt.

PRESIDENT THEODORE ROOSEVELT
From the famous portrait by John Singer Sargent, now in the White House.

William Emlen 1857-1930			Theodore 1858-1919 (26th President of the U. S.)			
George Emlen 1887-	John Kean 1889-	Philip James 1892-1941	Theodore, Jr. 1887-1944	Kermit 1889-1943	Archibald Bulloch 1894-	Quentin 1897-1918

CHAPTER VII.

WORLD WAR I—AND AFTERMATH

A FEW National Guard regiments off to camp . . . Red Cross parades in the city streets . . . Congress, working frantically in a reawakened Washington to establish a national conscription act weeks after the declaration of war . . . a whole nation trying desperately to make up for lost time.

That was the picture of America in 1917 as World War I caught the nation unprepared. Junker provocation had grown since President Wilson had been re-elected only five months previously, largely because he "kept us out of war," and there were few Americans who believed that our entry into the European conflict was inevitable and that we should take every step possible to prepare for it. But among those few, indeed their foremost spokesman, was Theodore Roosevelt.

This truly great citizen and ex-President had returned from Europe in 1911. Even then he had been sure that war in Europe was bound to come, and that, when it did, the United States could not stay out of it indefinitely. His position in life made an unqualified public assertion of these opinions inexpedient — there were many then, as later, to cry "warmonger" at men who were merely giving a sadly needed warning to the nation. He could, and did, stress publicly and often the need for armed preparedness; and in his own family he expressed his certainty that war would come.

George Emlen was among those who listened to "Cousin

73

Thee" and at once took a measure of personal preparedness by joining the Guard. This action was to lead to service on the Mexican Border, then to France and to high honor and responsibility in the first great conflict.

George Emlen was far from being the first Roosevelt to serve his country well in time of war, but earlier he had been a "first" in a very different respect. Although this line of the Roosevelts had been well-to-do, even wealthy, since the days of Johannes two centuries before, its elders, prior to William Emlen, stoutly maintained that a "practical education" was the proper preparation for a career in the firm. As a consequence, George was the first in the direct line of the heads of Roosevelt & Son to go to college!

To establish this precedent, George Emlen had to live up to three stringent conditions set by his father: that he be graduated before he was twenty-one, that he take honors in his studies while in college, and that he appear upon his graduation qualified by training to enter the firm. There were no "ifs" or "buts" about the requirements—and George Emlen met them by taking the four-year course at Harvard in three years, being graduated *cum laude* in mathematics, finding time to earn his varsity letter meanwhile, and entering the firm several months before the deadline.

It is not surprising that William Emlen had been so inflexible in this requirement, although a tolerant, kindly parent in most other respects. He had wanted to be a surgeon, but his sense of obligation to firm and family had led him to obey his father's wishes and renounce this ambition to enter Roosevelt & Son. Duty first—a Roosevelt characteristic. And now the pattern was to repeat itself, for George Emlen made so brilliant a record in mathematics at Harvard that he was assured of a full professorship if he would adopt an academic career. Mathematics was his supreme interest, but his father wanted him in the firm—and so, again, *duty first*. Mathematics was to remain George Emlen's avocation, however—a fact that was to have interesting consequences many years later in World War II, when his talents were put to work by the savants of his alma mater to evolve mathematical formulae used in creating the atomic bomb!

Back in 1914, however, young soldiers rather than scientists were in primary demand. The records show that George Roosevelt rose steadily in rank until, at the time of our entry into the war, he held a Majority in the National Guard; later, he rose to be Chief of Staff of the celebrated Eighty-second Division, being assigned to this post before his thirty-second birthday. Cousin Theodore's words had, indeed, been heard to advantage.

The two other sons of William Emlen also served throughout the war. John Kean, the second son, joined Naval Aviation, a branch then still in its infancy, and saw active service. He had resigned from the Officer's Reserve Corps, where he had little chance for action, to take this step.

Philip James, the youngest, had left the paths which most of the Roosevelts of this line had trodden in civilian life. He had been a newspaperman in his early youth, and later had taken up aviation, studying and writing about the new world of the air. Naturally, he was drawn to military aviation even before war broke out, but his eyesight was so bad that it was with difficulty that he got into the service at all.

If the medical authorities were liberal in their examination, they acted wisely as the event proved, for Captain Philip Roosevelt was responsible more than any other individual for developing daytime bombing — proving its feasibility to the dubious French and British. Later, he was decorated by the French for his part in the battles of the Meuse and the Marne. And one tragic day he saw his cousin, Lt. Quentin Roosevelt, the brilliant youngest son of Theodore Roosevelt, hurled from the skies in his bullet-riddled plane.

All of the sons of Theodore, like all of the sons of William Emlen, fought in that war — as did Roosevelts of other branches of the family. Only Quentin gave his life, although several were wounded, among them Col. Theodore Roosevelt, Jr., who served with bravery and distinction, and Archibald B. Roosevelt, who was discharged as 100 per cent disabled.

With peace, the three sons returned to civil life — Philip James joining George Emlen in Roosevelt & Son, and John Kean going with Central and South American Cables, later rising to be Chief Engineer. Here he was to continue for many years, and when the system was acquired by All-America Cables, he retained the post. As Chief Engineer he was responsible for the great network of cables that links all countries in the continent to the South with each other and with the United States.

William Emlen Roosevelt was still the head of Roosevelt & Son, and would so continue almost until his death in 1930. But George Emlen and Philip were to give a new orientation to Roosevelt & Son — or rather once more to bring its primary function in line with the tendencies of the day — even during their father's lifetime. And in this they were, like their predecessors, strictly in the tradition of the firm, pre-

One of the last portraits of General Theodore Roosevelt, Jr., who distinguished himself in two wars.

Facade of the Roosevelt Memorial Building
Named in commemoration of President Theodore Roosevelt, great
friend of the nation's natural resources and wild life.

serving the advantages of continuity while being responsive to proven ideas and techniques.

The direction which the firm now took was in the direction of *conservation*. This was, of course, no new thing for Roosevelt & Son, which had been responsible for the protection of the funds of members of its own family, of institutions and of others for a century and more. The differences, however, were two — first, that conservation, the intelligent management of invested capital, became the *primary business* of the firm and its partners, and second, that this evolution coincided with the evolution of America into a nation very different from that in which the Roosevelts of other generations had lived and worked.

We need not trace all the ramifications of the changing American economy since 1918. We know that the United States emerged from the war permanently a creditor nation; that a boom followed; that the worst depression in American history followed that; that all kinds of new restrictions on business and finance, many evolved from the very growing complexity of the modern world, others of an at least controversial character, then became the order of the day; and that, finally, our most costly, if victorious, war was to take place.

Naturally, the Roosevelts did not foresee all these developments. In 1924 the curtain was yet to rise on the more spectacular of them, but the overture was being played, and in its *leitmotif* could be heard, even then, the advent of an era of change, an age in which successful management of funds was to be, more than ever, a highly specialized occupation; an age in which "common sense," and "business judgment" would not alone be enough.

In 1924, therefore, under the sponsorship of Roosevelt & Son, Investment Managers Company was formed to specialize in fundamental research and investment analysis. Edgar Lawrence Smith, an established investment analyst, was among those who participated in the organization. At about this time he completed a monumental work entitled "Common Stocks as Long Term Investments." Mr. Smith had undertaken this study originally to demonstrate that, considered over a period of decades, bonds were superior to equities as measured by ultimate results. His studies indicated just the opposite, however; they showed rather that the growth of the country was roughly paralleled by common stocks.

To translate this conclusion into action was natural for a firm such as Roosevelt & Son. Accordingly, an investment fund was started, the assets of which, at inception, consisted of the personal investments of the sponsors of Investment Managers Company, which launched this comparatively early precursor of the many investment companies to follow. As public funds were attracted, two other investment companies were introduced under the same sponsorship. All three subsequently were merged into one company called Investors Management Fund, Inc.

By late 1933 the growing complexities of the management of money, including the advent of Leftist trends in government, *de facto* abandonment of the gold standard and the world-wide depression, made concentration on this one task of conservation advisable. Accordingly, in that year Roosevelt & Son abandoned its investment banking activities and henceforth confined its activities to the management of funds and trusts in its care. Again we see the firm and its partners anticipating what has since become a major tendency in the field of business and finance — management of money as a full-time task.

In 1939, Investors Management Company, Inc., as it was now called, took an even more significant step when it acquired the management contract of Fundamental Investors, Inc., an investment company, from E. A. Pierce & Company. Philip James Roosevelt became President, and on taking office remarked whimsically:

"I will make but two promises. I will be honest and I shall make mistakes."

This modest approach was characteristic of the man and the firm. Philip Roosevelt was a man who, steeped in the tradition of the firm, never hesitated to take an original viewpoint if his experience, training and judgment told him it was the right one. For instance, the following quotation from a letter he wrote to a business associate, in May, 1941, when almost everyone was pessimistic, reflects these qualities:

"I was only six years old when my grandfather died, yet I can remember quite clearly his sitting with my father on the porch of his home at Oyster Bay and saying that his business acts which had ended most successfully had apparently been actuated by charitable motives. His words were somewhat as follows:

" 'When nobody wanted property and everyone wanted to sell, if I helped them out by buying, it seems to have been a good idea; and in the same way, if nobody wanted to sell and everybody wanted to buy, my experience has been that it was wise to be charitable and help them out by selling.'

"I wonder if it might be not only the charitable but also

the successfully selfish thing to buy a few good stocks today when, measured by the old yardsticks, they are cheap."

Fundamental Investors, while important as constituting a modern type of investment vehicle, was but one of the many conservation activities of Roosevelt & Son — by this time rated as the oldest trust and estate management firm in the city. In addition to the large estates of which members of the firm were trustees, Roosevelt & Son was active in banking, industry and commerce. In real estate alone Roosevelt & Son is reputed to have had interests in no less than thirty-nine states at this time. The "mistakes" could not have been many.

When Philip James Roosevelt died in 1941, just one month before Pearl Harbor, he was an officer, Trustee or Director of upward of twenty banks, insurance companies, utilities, railroads and other enterprises. This, of course, was quite apart from the activities of George Emlen Roosevelt, by this time the head of the firm, and of John Kean Roosevelt.

Upon Philip Roosevelt's death, Philip W. K. Sweet, a long-time associate, became President, and George Emlen took office as Chairman of the Board of Investors Management Company. Then came Pearl Harbor, and the firm began a new chapter of its long history.

CHAPTER VIII.

GEORGE EMLEN ROOSEVELT
Fifth and present head of Roosevelt & Son,
in his office at 30 Pine Street.

CHAPTER VIII.

AN OLD TRADITION
AND THE NEW YORK OF 1946

NEW YORK, the New Amsterdam of the first Roosevelts, the "Bagdad on the Subway" of O. Henry, the city so often thought of in connection with the theatre and the night club, has another side of which few, even of those who spend their lives in it, are fully aware. Actually, the percentage of the eight million souls now cramming the city who gain their daily bread in the entertainment business is about as important as, say, the number of cab drivers in London or *café chanteuse* employes in prewar Paris. And, by the same token, the Manhattan playboys whose tabloid careers are apparently the sole objects of their lives are as important to the fundamental life of the city as were the less reputable of the British nobility to the Empire's capital, or as was the *boulevardier* to the quondam City of Light.

It is the unfortunate destiny of each of these cities to be judged, more often than not, by these flamboyant symbols. Yet, a thousand-fold more important, in each city there exists the working, every-day world, a community which is the real reason for any city's greatness.

Who, for instance, of those who have frequented the *purlieus* of 52nd Street, would guess that tucked between two night clubs is a spark plug factory that daily employs more than 2,500 people? Yet this kind of example could be extended indefinitely—with the result that New York is the leading industrial city in the country, although seldom thought of as industrial at all.

And in the world of finance there is again the same parallel. There are the figures who flash up, make national headlines and skyrocket out. And there are those who, like the Roosevelts, are a part of the sinew and backbone of the basic financial structure of America.

For New York today—the New York of Roosevelt & Son— is the center of financial, business and even general economic research. So extensive has this necessary work become in the complex modern world that it forms a business, an industry in its own right.

There are reasons, realized by few. One is that the executive offices of many large corporations are largely concentrated in New York City and this, in turn, makes the top executives of these companies more accessible to those in New York who seek information concerning their activities.

As a center of world trade, New York offers analysts many opportunities to keep their fingers on the pulse of global industrial conditions—through exporters and importers, companies with large foreign business and, perhaps most important, the large international banks. These same banks also afford a means, through their own extensive research departments, of getting information otherwise difficult to assemble from all parts of the United States.

To what extent these great financial institutions are concentrated in New York can be gleaned by a glance at some figures. Seven of the ten largest banks, twelve of the first twenty, are located in New York. Among the insurance companies,

Photograph by Fairchild Aerial Surveys, Inc.

NEW YORK'S DOWNTOWN DISTRICT
Center of the nation's financial and economic
research activities.

A typical mid-day scene on New Street, immediately behind the New York Stock Exchange.

Courtesy of Mr. Gardner Osborn

which likewise maintain huge research and investment departments, ten of the twenty largest fire and casualty companies, just half, have their main offices in New York — as do seven of twenty largest casualty and surety companies and four of the top twenty life companies. And about as many maintain their main offices in Hartford, Connecticut, a short ride from Manhattan.

Basic source material is likewise concentrated in New York. The files of the New York Public Library, for example, contain more actual economic data than those of any other institution in the United States. Important, too, is the fact that the New York Federal Reserve Bank Bulletin and the Reserve Board publications compiled and edited in the city reflect official statistics gathered in the area.

In the matter of news, financial newspapers and publications are concentrated in New York for the same reasons analysts are — and while their business is the gathering and dissemination of financial news for national consumption, their staffs and their files are themselves often a readily available source of needed facts.

Another aspect: about half of the larger national economic research organizations maintain their headquarters in Manhattan — organizations such as the National Industrial Conference Board, the Twentieth Century Fund and the National Bureau of Economic Research. Likewise, the major statistical services are to a great extent located in New York — and, as an indication of how large these activities are, one of them alone employs over 1,000 people in gathering, correlating and producing information concerning business prospects in general and individual enterprises in particular.

Again, because New York has been, as we have seen, the financial center of the country ever since there has been an American finance in the modern sense, most firms doing a financial business have their main offices in the city. A firm like Roosevelt & Son, for example, could hardly have had an exactly similar career in any other part of the country. The result is that, as these firms do more business here, they can afford to maintain staffs commensurate with their responsibilities.

There is another reason why research has grown in importance in New York. It is because there has been a vital need for competent men to digest and interpret the mass of investment information that the government and the organized exchanges require of corporations, the securities of which are offered to the public or which are "listed."

Thus the world of George Emlen Roosevelt as the head of Roosevelt & Son is very different from that of "C.V.S." It is even different, in regard to the necessity for financial research, from the earlier world of the last preceding head of the house, William Emlen Roosevelt. For New York is today the center of research in the same way that Detroit is the capital of the automobile world, Boston the center of the wool trade, Philadelphia is identified with carpet manufacture and Los Angeles is the heart of the motion picture industry.

This has led to what is, in nature and scope, virtually a unique organization, the New York Society of Security Analysts.

Before this group appear at regular intervals many of the leading industrialists of the country. In 1945, during the last quarter alone, the Society was addressed by top executive

Photograph by John Warren Wright

WALL STREET TODAY

The light building at the left is the New York Stock Exchange. Compare it and today's Trinity Church building with previous structures shown on pages 40 and 12. In the right foreground is the Bank of New York building (for comparison, see pages 26 and 27).

officers of such companies as Yale & Towne, Chrysler, Continental Oil, United Drug, Time, Inc., Commercial Credit, Johns-Manville, and American Radiator. Leading editors, economists, two government officials, and the former British Ambassador to Moscow also addressed the membership during the year. This wasn't unusual—it was at least typical.

Beyond all this, however, is the fact that through interchange of views of members, by personal contact and through the publication of its own quarterly Journal, the Society has brought into being a community within a community. It is not unlike a body of industrial scientists working in the same general area, banded together to further their discoveries. And each year since 1935, this work has become more important with the growing complexity of industry, finance and government regulation. For this reason, investment analysts in other parts of the country, especially in the East, make occasional trips to New York to attend the meetings of the Society and discuss matters of mutual interest with members and others concerned with investment.

The significance of this background in relation to the present activities of Roosevelt & Son—which now is trustee for, or manages, funds believed to be in excess of $100,000,000 —is very real. Actually the firm's main interest and business today—the management of invested funds—involves continuous contact with this world.

For George Emlen this contact is assured by a wide acquaintance among leaders of finance and industry and through almost daily association with Board members of Investors Management Company and the investment companies it serves. In addition to Philip Sweet, who is a member of the Society, these directors include such men as John F. B. Mitchell and John J. Whipple, partners of Wood, Walker & Company, a well-known investment house; Amory Houghton, Chairman, and Arthur Houghton, a Director, of Corning Glass Works; George M. Grinnell, the partner in charge of research of Dick & Merle-Smith, an investment firm of national repute; Allan L. Melhado, a financial advisor to several large corporations, and General Boykin C. Wright of Shearman & Sterling & Wright, legal counsel to the National City Bank of New York and other large financial institutions and corporations.

The management of invested funds is, of course, only one of the wide interests of the present head of Roosevelt & Son. Several of these responsibilities are inherited, such as the Presidency of the Broadway Improvement Society (the family real estate holding company) and the directorship of many large hotels. Among the many other corporations of which he is a director, it is notable that he serves on the Board of the Union Pacific Railroad, which his grandfather, James Alfred, helped finance. He served as a Director of the Chemical Bank until he resigned in favor of his brother, John Kean, who recently became a partner in the firm — the fifth Roosevelt to be a Director of the Chemical.

In addition to these posts, however, George Roosevelt has been sought for his own abilities by many of the large institutions of the city and country. To mention but a few of his activities, he serves on the Board of the Guaranty Trust Company; he is Chairman of the Executive Committee of the great Bank for Savings in the City of New York; he serves as an Arbitrator of the American Arbitration Association.

In the field of real estate, George Roosevelt was called upon to help in many of the difficult situations that followed the collapse of the Florida land boom in 1926, and in the national decline in real estate values following 1930. In this capacity he serves, or has served, as a director of, or trustee in, the reorganization of at least 165 major properties in various parts of the country, almost all of which by now have been successfully liquidated or re-established on a sound basis.

Outside of business and finance, George Emlen continues the family tradition of close association with Roosevelt Hospital, serving as Vice-President and Trustee, and is Treasurer of the New York Dispensary. A versatile man, his manifold activities range from the Presidency of the Marshall Chess Club and membership on the Visiting Committee of the Mathematics Department at Harvard (on which he has served for thirty-three years) to an almost unprecedented term of four years as Commodore of the New York Yacht Club.

The latter connection is interesting. When war came to the United States a second time in the life of this generation of the Roosevelts of Oyster Bay, George Emlen was about to begin his first year as Commodore, to which he had been elected largely because of his accomplishment as a practical transatlantic yachtsman and cup racer. Our Navy desperately needed help in searching for U-boats, particularly around the approaches to New York Harbor. The membership of the New York Yacht Club, almost en masse, served as auxiliaries of the Navy in this work—and, although the work involved very real dangers, not a man or a boat was lost in the entire war.

George Roosevelt himself was offered commissions in the Army, Navy and Coast Guard, but, realizing that his age—

The original ledger of James I Roosevelt, founder of Roosevelt
& Son, still preserved in the office of the old firm.

A corner of the office of Roosevelt & Son today. Note the
old wooden safe, still in use by Walter Nestel, an assistant to the partners.

he was in his early fifties—made it likely that he would have mainly desk work to do, he felt that he could be of greater service and have more freedom of action as a civilian. The results of this choice showed in his work in connection with the atomic bomb, mentioned earlier, and in the classes in navigation which he conducted and through which hundreds of young Navy men passed.

Both his sons and those of his brother, John Kean, served in the Army and Navy, joining the sons of the other Roosevelts on the world battlefields where victory was wrought. General Theodore Roosevelt, Jr., fell in France and Major Kermit Roosevelt died in Alaska. The surviving son of President Theodore Roosevelt, Archibald Bulloch, is probably the only living man who was discharged from both World Wars as 100 per cent disabled in each case. "Archy" Roosevelt, too, makes his present business headquarters at Roosevelt & Son.

It is from the ranks of the sons of George, John and Philip that the future head of the firm of Roosevelt & Son will come. These sons constitute the tenth generation of Roosevelts in America—and those who become associated with Roosevelt & Son will represent the sixth generation in the firm. A century and a half—through which, as we have seen, the history of the firm has been virtually that of the history of the country. A century and a half — coming down in direct descent, without any outside interests — for the firm, never having had to seek outside financing in spite of all the wars, panics, booms and depressions through which it has passed, has remained a family entity.

Yes, whoever eventually succeeds George Emlen Roosevelt as head of the firm will, we may be sure, have been thoroughly imbued with a sense of tradition, of integrity and of continuity so well summed up in the motto of the family, "Qui Plantavit Curabit," emblazoned on its coat of arms:

"The one who planted it will take care of it."

QUI PLANTAVIT CURABIT

BIBLIOGRAPHY

Cyclopaedia of American Biography. New York: D. Appleton & Co., 1888.

National Cyclopaedia of American Biography. New York: James T. White & Co., 1898.

New York Genealogical & Biographical Record, The. April 1933; Jan. 1941.

"Pioneers and Founders of New Netherland: Claes Martenszen Van Rosenvelt." *New Netherland Register.* New York, 1911. 80 v.i., pp. 8-11.

Roosevelt Genealogy, 1649-1902, The. Hartford: C. B. Whittelsey (c. 1902). 121 pp.

Some Historical Notes of the Early Days of the Bank for Savings in the City of New York. 1944.

BARRETT, WALTER (J. A. Scoville). *The Old Merchants of New York City.* 5 vols. 1885.

EARLE, ALICE M. *Colonial Days in Old New York.* New York: Empire State Book Co. (c. 1896). 312 pp.

FISKE, STEPHEN. *Offhand Portraits of Famous New Yorkers.* 1884.

HART, SMITH. *The New Yorkers; the Story of a People and Their City.* New York: Sheridan House (c. 1938). 253 pp.

KIRKLAND, EDWARD C. *History of American Economic Life.* New York: F. S. Crofts & Co., 1939. 810 pp.

LEONARD, JOHN W. "History of the City of New York, 1609-1909." *Journal of Commerce and Commercial Bulletin.* New York, 1910.

OSBORN, GARDNER. *The Streets of Old New York.* New York: Harper & Brothers, 1939.

PARTRIDGE, BELLAMY. *An Imperial Saga.* New York: Hillman-Curl, Inc., 1936. Pp. xvi, 11, 19, 325.

PICKARD, M. FORTESCUE. *The Roosevelts and America.* London: H. Joseph, Ltd., 1941. Pp. 11, 17, 288.

PRINGLE, HENRY F. *Theodore Roosevelt: A Biography.* 1931.

ROOSEVELT, THEODORE. *New York.* New York: Longmans, Green & Co., 1895. 232 pp.

SABINE, LORENZO. *Biographical Sketches of the Loyalists in the American Revolution.* 2 vols. 1864.

SCHIFTGIESSER, KARL. *The Amazing Roosevelt Family, 1613-1943.* New York: W. Funk, Inc., 1942. XII, 367 pp.

STOKES, I. N. P. *The Iconography of Manhattan Island.*

VALENTINE, DAVID T. *History of the City of New York.* New York: G. P. Putnam & Co., 1853. Pp. 7, 404.

WEEKS, LYMAN HORACE. *Prominent Families of New York.* 1897.

19 46

This book was designed by R. L. Harrison and
produced entirely by offset lithography under the
direction of William E. Rudge's Sons, New York City.
Type face is Baskerville, Roman and Italic.
Binding is by Russell-Rutter Company, Inc.,
New York City

Date Due

		PRINTED IN U. S. A.	